4

Kauai Travel Guide

The Most Up-To-Date Pocket Guide To Discover Kauai's Hidden Treasures | Plan the Most Beautiful Trip to the Astonish Garden Island and Visit It Like a Local

Nigel Christopher

consult a licensed professional before attempting any techniques outlined in this book.

By reading this document, the reader agrees that under no circumstances is the author responsible for any direct or indirect losses incurred due to the use of the information contained within this document, including, but not limited to, errors, omissions, or inaccuracies.

Table of Contents

Introduction

Let's start by making the pronunciation clear: It can be spelled either "Kauai" or "Kaua'i," with the apostrophe denoting a third syllable, because it can be pronounced either ka-WAI or ka-WAH-ee.

A Polynesian navigator named Kawai'iloa, who originated in... Polynesia, is said to have discovered the Hawaiian Islands. His three sons were Maui, O'ahu, and Kaua'i. His favorite island was Kaua'i.

The word "place about the neck" is in the name itself. This alludes to the way a father carries his beloved child, with the youngster's arms encircling his neck, or something.

Kawai is the oldest of Hawaii's main islands from a geological perspective, which likely explains why they had a head start on making it right. This place is known as the "Garden Isle" and the "Island of Discovery" for a reason. It's simply that lovely!

Kauai was created by volcanoes, just as all the other islands. This one has had almost six million years to create its hilly topography. With a height of around 5,243 feet, Kawaikini is the tallest of these, while Wai'ale'ale, which is close to the island's center, is the second highest.

Due to the quantity of rain it gets each year, the latter peak has the unfortunate distinction of being one of the wettest places on planet. The rain has sculpted a breathtaking environment with soaring canyons and waterfalls throughout the last millennium. The Waimea Canyon State Park, often known as the "Grand Canyon of the Pacific," is the most breathtaking of these. It resembles the Grand Canyon as well, albeit in a much greener and wetter form.

With only 69,512 inhabitants as of the 2013 census, Kauai is not the most populous of Hawaii's islands despite its breathtaking nature. Some claim that there are actually more wild chickens on the island than people. These hens were introduced by the first Polynesian immigrants and have thrived due to the lack of natural predators on the island.

However, this does not imply that there is only chicken to be eaten on the island. Not at all. The island's top three industries are tourism, government, and retail. Therefore, this travel guide ebook will inform you about the top locations for dining, drinking, and sightseeing.

Though even by the standards of the US mainland, Kauai (like the rest of the Hawaiian Islands) is not inexpensive. This is because a large portion of what the state consumes is not produced locally. A much of its food, transportation, and technology are imported, which raises the cost of everything else. Apart from that, there are a variety of possibilities based on your budget. So that you may start traveling, let's start reading!

Chapter 1:
Things you must know
about Kauai.

Here are some crucial details about Kauai that you should be aware of if you're thinking about visiting:

The fourth-largest Hawaiian island, Kauai is situated in the center of the Pacific Ocean. It belongs to the American state of Hawaii.

Geographically speaking, Kauai, sometimes known as the "Garden Isle," is a stunningly gorgeous island with lush jungles, cliffs, waterfalls, and beaches. The Hawaiian chain's oldest and northernmost island is this one.

Climate: The tropical climate in Kauai has generally stable temperatures all year long. With typical temperatures ranging from 70°F (21°C) to 85°F (29°C), prepare for warm and humid weather. Rain is a possibility occasionally, especially on the north shore.

Popular Attractions: There are numerous attractions and activities available on Kauai. The Napali Coast, Waimea Canyon, Hanalei Bay, Wailua Falls, and Poipu Beach are some of the must-see locations. Waimea Canyon is also referred to as the "Grand Canyon of the Pacific."

Outdoor Recreation: Kauai is a haven for nature lovers. Hiking along beautiful pathways, paddling or kayaking on the Wailua River, snorkeling or scuba diving in bright coral reefs, and even zip-lining through lush forests are all enjoyable activities.

Na Pali Coast: One of Kauai's most recognizable landmarks is the Na Pali Coast. It has stunning cliffs, underwater caverns, and undiscovered beaches. While you can stroll some of the coast, a boat tour or a helicopter ride are two of the more common ways to see it.

Hanalei: The north shore village of Hanalei is renowned for its scenic scenery and laid-back atmosphere. It provides access to lovely stores, eateries, and stunning beaches like Hanalei Bay.

Safety precautions: The island of Kauai's natural environment may be both breathtaking and dangerous. When exploring coastal locations, hiking trails, or taking part in water activities, pay close attention to safety precautions. Keep up with the weather and be ready for unforeseen developments.

Local Culture: The history of the island of Kauai is closely entwined with the island's vibrant Hawaiian culture. Consider learning a few Hawaiian words and phrases to show respect for the local traditions and customs.

Environmentalism: Kauai's natural beauty should be respected, so engage in eco-friendly travel. Take nothing from the beaches or natural areas, respect the delicate ecosystems, and properly dispose of your garbage.

To make the most of your stay on the island, remember to plan your vacation in advance, investigate any travel limitations or prerequisites, and have a flexible schedule. Have fun when visiting Kauai!

Chapter 2:
Kauai Essentials.

Best times to visit Kauai.

In terms of weather, crowds, demand, and costs, the months of April, May, August, September, October, and November are the ideal periods to visit Kauai.

Although visitors looking for a winter getaway aren't deterred by Kauai's rainy season, which runs from November to March, you should be aware that costs will rise dramatically because this is the busiest time of year for tourists.

The season normally lasts from January until spring, so if you're interested in whale watching, now is the time to go. If you find winter to be too pricey, think about the spring and fall seasons as a compromise: Prices in Kauai slightly decrease during these off-peak periods.

While it won't be as expensive as it is in the winter, traveling to Kauai in the summer won't be considerably less expensive either.

September-November (Best time to visit) (Perfect time to go)

Once the summer tourists have left, many hotels offer reduced fall prices. You'll also run into less visitors as you explore. Expect lows to remain in the upper sixties and highs in the mid- to low-eighties.

Crucial Occasions

Kauai's Mokihana Festival (September)

Kauai marathon (September)

Kauai's Festival of Chocolate and Coffee (October)

December-March

The bulk of visitors to Kauai arrive during this time to avoid the cooler weather elsewhere because this is when the island has its roughest weather. The average amount of precipitation is very high, especially in December. If you want to avoid a lot of moisture, spend your vacation on the drier west and south coastlines. You shouldn't stress too much about the weather ruining your plans, though. In Kauai, downpours rarely last for days or even hours, but rather just a few minutes. Make reservations several weeks to months in advance if you intend to visit during this time because it is the island's biggest travel season.

Crucial Occasions

Town of Waimea Festival (February)

A celebration of Prince Kuhio (March)

April-June (Best time to visit) (Perfect time to go)

Springtime temperatures on Kauai are picture-perfect (highs in the high 70s and low 80s), and hotel rates are affordable (this period is considered a low season). Around the fewest crowds, schedule your trip for early spring, before the summer season begins.

Crucial Occasions

Kauai hosts an art fair (June)

July-August

Summertime family trips coincide with price rises at Kauai hotels. If you're itching for a summer vacation, keep in mind that you'll need to make reservations long in advance and that you can expect to pay around the same as you would for a winter vacation. This time of year is hard to pass up because the weather is perfect for heading to the beach, with highs in the mid-80s and lows in the mid-70s.

Crucial Occasions

In the past, Koloa Plantation (July)

There are Kauai Shrimp Dumplings available at The Kauai Grill at The St. Regis Princeville Resort.

This dish of tender dumplings stuffed with just caught shrimp is the definition of comfort food. The lobster sauce, ginger, and shiitake mushrooms that are presented with it give each bite a flavorful punch.

Respect

As with other forms of travel, it's crucial to be adaptable, courteous, and open-minded. Keep in mind that the indigenous culture is still very much in existence. There are numerous locations that appear to be undeveloped beauty areas but are actually sacred sites that are clearly identified with signage. Locals would be offended if you disrespected a holy spot in the same way as Christians would feel enraged to see church grounds desecrated.

Safety

The state's search and rescue teams record an annual increase in the number of operations they have to mount despite the island's breathtaking beauty. Non-Hawaiian tourists who neglect paths or simply have to jump into that tempting body of water account for a disproportionately large number of missing, hurt, or stranded hikers. Before beginning any hike or swim, download the free Hiking Safety in Hawaii booklet from the state's website at www.hawaiistateparks.org/brochures.

Marijuana and Nudism

The two most widespread misconceptions about Hawaii are that marijuana is legal and that nudists can bathe on public beaches. Although Kauai's climate is perfect for producing pot, the state abides by federal law, thus getting found with it will result in punishment. Public nudity is likewise prohibited.

Driving

Because everyone on the island is so laid back, drivers respect other people's right of way and do not block traffic or turn left. You will be required to extend the same courtesy. Since honking is so disrespectful, it is rarely done.

Directions

On Kauai, the cardinal points are of limited use, therefore directions are dependent on the topography. Makai and mauka both refer to the sea or a mountain, respectively. These two points of reference are used regardless of where you are on the island or which road you are on.

Kauai's nightlife

The tropical setting, climate, beaches, and local cuisine of Kauai make it an especially well-liked island. Its nightlife is not very well known, though. The roadways of Kauai, a mostly rural Hawaiian island, are typically cleared before midnight. There usually isn't enough regular commerce to support a downtown late-night sector without a large population of young residents. There are a few places to go out at night, but they aren't nearly as numerous as the beaches or the places to catch shrimp. The majority of the island's nightlife may be found during luau performances and island meals. Hotel lounges and resorts are frequently the finest places to hear live music, however some bars and eateries also offer late-night entertainment.

The Stevenson's Library is a popular late-night hangout. Stevenson's Library, which is housed in the Hyatt Regency Hotel, boasts dark wood paneling and a relaxed ambiance. There is a bar that serves a wide range of island beverages and can get rather crowded with tourists and other island visitors. Customers are also given access to premium cigars, a free pool table, and other amenities. Jazz bands frequently perform at Stevenson's, contributing to the lounge's relaxed atmosphere.

The Shack, a different nightlife location, is located in Kapaa town. A bar with an American vibe is called The Shack. It offers a variety of drinks and foods, with nachos being a particular favorite.

One of Hanalei's more well-known locations is Tahiti Nui. The decor is cheerful and laid-back with some locally produced art. Tahiti Nui is the ideal location for a nightcap or some karaoke because of the cozy ambience. Dancing is prevalent, and sometimes local musicians provide the background music.

Bar Acuda is a brand-new, stylish bar on the north coast that offers guests a chic setting for wine and dining. It's easy to understand why it's become a popular destination because it remains open longer than most restaurants and offers unusual meals like lobster-stuffed squid.

Keoki's Paradise, located in Koloa's Poipu Shopping Village, is another hip and stylish location. Keoki's Paradise is an outdoor pub that is illuminated by tiki torches that are placed all around it. For those who like to spend their time drinking and mingling with other customers, it's a terrific hangout place. There are Hawaiian music dance floors and live musicians.

If you want to enjoy the nightlife, Kauai has some terrific options overall. But compared to what most people would encounter on the mainland, the late-night atmosphere is far less varied and intense. Most people in Kauai prefer to take advantage of the late hours by going for a walk on the beach or having a quick drink at the hotel bar. There are numerous possibilities available to you if you decide to spend the night somewhere other than your hotel.

Things to Pack for Kauai

The island of Kauai is designed for comfort and relaxation. On vacation, it's common to be unsure of what to bring. However, if you're traveling to Kauai, you can unwind because packing will be simple. Some of the essentials are listed below.

Put away the formal attire first. You won't need those because Kauai's atmosphere is so relaxed. Next, grab a pair of sunglasses because Kauai has year-round sunny and tropical weather. Wearing sunglasses can protect your eyes from the sun's glare and keep you comfortable while traveling. You should wear proper clothing because Kauai's climate is so tropical. You'll perspire and feel uncomfortable with long pants and tight clothing. Shorts, t-shirts, and loose-fitting apparel that will keep you cool as you traverse the island are things you should pack. Another excellent option is sunscreen since the sun is always shining and a sunburn may ruin any holiday. A camera is the final item you'll need. When visiting an island like Kauai, you should always take pictures to save your memories. If you intend to participate in any beach activities, ensure that your camera can withstand water. You can continue to enjoy the moment even after you leave the island with the aid of a decent camera.

After you've packed the essentials, there are a few other items you should acquire to add a little more enjoyment to your Kauai vacation. Most of these items are transportable, while some will be bought on the island. A water bottle is the most crucial of these goods. In Kauai, it's simple to become overheated by the sun, and becoming dehydrated can ruin any island getaway. On the island, hiking may be pretty strenuous and there is a ton of beautiful scenery. Water isn't always available, and it's not always safe to consume the water from lakes and streams. Therefore, it is essential to have a water bottle with you when exploring Kauai. Then comes a map. Maps of the island that may be purchased in Kauai include tourist attractions as well as all the roads and walkways. Planning your days becomes quick and simple as a result. The last item on the list of things you should probably carry is bug spray. You'll be spending a lot of time outside, and tropical climates are where mosquitoes and other insects thrive. Bug spray is a must if you don't want to be bothered by and swatting at mosquitoes.

The final point relates to accessories. Although you probably won't need them, you could wish to bring them depending on the activities you want to engage in while on the island. You might want to bring snorkeling equipment if you plan to spend a lot of time at the beach or scuba diving. You'll be able to swim farther down comfortably as a result. Given the wide variety of activities available on the island, you might also wish to bring a few pairs of various shoes. Although flip-flops are excellent for walking, hiking boots would be preferable for a hike across the island. Make sure the shoes you bring aren't too fine because the island's red dirt can stain them with its crimson color.

On Kauai, it's crucial to maintain your comfort. And that implies that you don't need to travel far to have fun. Sunglasses, shorts, and sunscreen are essentials, and everything else will fall into place if you have those. You might wish to bring some of the other items on the list as well, depending on what you decide to accomplish while on the island. Make sure you have some of these goods when preparing for your trip to Kauai to increase the enjoyment of your stay.

Establishing a Budget

The estimated costs for the two components of your holiday are broken down below.

Between-island flights: $50 to $100

Renting a car costs $35 to $70 per day.

A shared dormitory bed costs $40 to $50 a night, a private Airbnb room costs $50 to $100, and a single room at a five-star hotel or beachfront resort costs $120 to $250 per night.

A restaurant lunch costs $15 to $30, with tax.

Luau shows go from $75 to $120.

For a 2-tank dive, the price ranges from $120 to $180 plus equipment expenditures.

Surfing lesson: $75

Spending: $100 to $250 (can be excluded to save for a budget-friendly trip)

Poke bowl: $12–$15

Fresh coconuts cost between $5 and $8; a trip to Hawaii wouldn't be complete without one!

These are some average travel expenses on Kauai. Your expectations and vacation goals may cause your spending plan to vary.

Local Custom Upon arrival, locals give each guest an affectionate "Aloha" and a lei, or traditional flower necklace. Leis should be worn closed with one half at the front and the other dangling down the back. If the lei is open or untied, let it dangle freely around your neck. When entering a Hawaiian's home, always leave your shoes or slippers at the door. When you visit, provide a gift, or omiyage, for the host. The locals will welcome your learning Hawaiian. Some of them are:

- mahalo: thank you
- e komo mai: welcome

- a hui hou: until we meet again
- kokua: help
- ono: delicious
- e kala mai i a`u: please forgive me (generally used for "I am sorry")

Ocean Safety and Marine Life Regulations

The Pacific is warm and alluring, but if you disregard warnings, it might endanger your life. If you can't swim, you must do this. Always look for a lifeguard on the beach before you enter the water. Residents and lifeguards will tell you not to turn your back on the water, so listen to them. If weather reports and beach signs warn you of hazardous conditions, stay out of the water. Since box jellyfish stings can cause serious rashes and edema, they should be avoided. Most importantly, stay your distance from marine life. Any level of human engagement or interference may be detrimental to aquatic life as well as you. Because it is illegal to feed, touch, or otherwise contact with marine life, you should always be courteous of it and stay a safe distance from it.

Travelling Kauai

One of the most important considerations before traveling to Hawaii is the transportation options. There are 8 islands in Hawaii, and because they are all far apart from one another, you must know how to get to the island of your choice.

By Air

If you wish to effectively hop islands, you have to fly across them. Hawaiian Airlines, Mokulele Airlines, and Southwest Airlines are a few of the main airlines that provide these condensed itineraries. The main hub for flights between islands and abroad is often Oahu. Flying to another island from Honolulu International Airport (HNL) takes 30 to 45 minutes. Unbelievably difficult to reach, the Forbidden Island of Niihau can only be traveled to and explored by helicopter. However, they might break the bank and spend a substantial amount of your money.

Even though ferries are a rare form of transportation, many services still connect Lanai and Maui. The 45- to 60-minute ride costs about $30 one way. Due to the low frequency of ferry service, you must make a reservation in advance. If you adore the sea and want to see the Pacific personally, ferries are a far better choice than airplanes. For a more luxurious experience, you can rent a boat to travel to the four main islands and stay the night.

Only the boat and the air are accessible for getting between islands when traveling by car. Once you reach an island, you can rent a vehicle and embark on a road trip. Even without a license, you can use the Oahu bus system, which covers most of the island. Just be careful to check the bus schedules to see whether you can travel to any desired locations by bus. You can also book a taxi or join a tour for a more leisurely experience.

To make packing easier, develop a list of all the equipment and supplies you'll need for your Hawaii vacation. Get a local map and mark the places on it that you will be visiting in advance. Always check the weather and make sure you have the proper equipment, but that is more important.

Top-Tips & Money-Saving Techniques

Due to the lengthy, pricey flights, the lodging, and even simply obtaining some food and drink, visiting the Hawaiian Islands may end up costing a lot of money overall. However, coming here on a shoestring budget is not difficult because there are many of ways you may save a ton of cash. Here are some of the best ways to minimize expenses without sacrificing the quality of your trip to the Hawaiian Islands.

After season One of the best ways to save money is to visit Kauai off-season when lodging is more cheaper, there are fewer people, and flights are much more affordable.

Avoid Too many trips are planned Before you even fly to Hawaii, it's a good idea to avoid overbooking in order to save money. Prior to your trip, it can be tempting to schedule and secure a ton of fun activities, but doing so can be expensive. Choose to book a few rooms in advance instead of all of them, and then book the rest when you get there.

Eat Locally - Eating like a local is one of the best things you can do when visiting the islands if you're a true foodie and are on a tight budget. This means finding the best eateries in each location after learning more about it. Compared to the normal tourist trap restaurants, these will likely be both far more inexpensive and delicious.

Eating at home If you don't care much about eating out and trying different foods, renting an apartment or staying in a hostel with a kitchen are alternative options for saving money. By doing this, you can make your own meals at a far lower cost by buying the ingredients at the grocery store.

Don't Be Careless - Avoid the same mistake that many island visitors do by avoiding dangerous waters and hiking trails. This can result in extremely expensive hospital bills that could have been avoided.

Free Things - One of the best ways to save money and still have a good time on Kauai is to take advantage of the free activities the island has to offer. These include activities like going on hikes, strolling along the beach, and watching sunsets. To have a good time, you don't always need to spend a lot of money on entertainment.

Be Flexible - Before you even depart for Kauai, consider being flexible with your travel dates. Unless you can only travel during the summer vacation season, being flexible can help you find some excellent ticket and accommodation discounts.

Consider Travel Package Reservations - Another option that is frequently substantially less expensive than doing everything separately is booking a package trip that includes transportation, accommodation, and flights. You are relieved of the stress, and your expenses may go down dramatically.

Although it is not always possible, traveling in a large group is a fantastic and entertaining way to save money when visiting Kauai. It frequently lowers the cost of lodging as well as transportation, such as car rentals or even taxis.

On every island, there are both more expensive and touristy regions and less expensive and more local areas. Avoid staying in the more touristic districts. A great way to reduce costs is to stay away from popular tourist destinations and in more remote places. This is a great approach to experience the islands because it feels much more genuine.

Make a financial plan in advance. Research choices like TripAdvisor ahead to get an idea of what to expect in terms of price and quality rather than blowing your budget at the first upscale restaurant you see. Before you even go for the islands, determine how much money you want to spend overall and break it down by day in order to be prepared and economical with your expenditures.

Have a Picnic on the Beach - Finding creative ways to spend your time and money are excellent ways to save expenditures without compromising the overall experience. Instead of paying a premium for a coastal restaurant, take a picnic lunch to the beach. You can buy your groceries at the supermarket and take them with you to the beach.

Stay on just one island. If you are planning a cheap trip to Hawaii but won't be staying there for an extended period of time, one option is to stay on one island rather than visiting all of them. It could be wiser to concentrate on one and take a shorter, less expensive route because the flights between them are so pricey.

Employer or Volunteer? If you wish to extend your stay, securing temporary job in the Hawaiian Islands is a great option. You can do this to get money while simultaneously exploring and taking full advantage of island living. A fulfilling and pleasurable way to spend your time is to volunteer for particular groups like charity in exchange for meals and housing.

Tipping

Tipping is a typical custom and a significant component of the service sector on Kauai, as it is throughout much of the United States. Although it is not required, tipping is typically accepted as usual for a variety of services. The typical rules for tipping in Kauai are as follows:

Restaurants: Before any reductions or taxes, it is usual to tip between 15 and 20 percent of the total amount. Before leaving a bigger group an additional tip, it's a good idea to check the bill as some establishments may automatically add a service charge. You might think about tipping more if you experienced great service or went to a high-end restaurant.

Bars: If you're running a tab, it's typical to give the bartender $1 to $2 each drink or 15 to 20 percent of the overall tab.

Hotels: Tipping is customary at hotels. Depending on the hotel and the degree of service, you can offer the cleaning workers a tip, which is often in the range of $2 to $5 daily. In addition, it is usual to tip staff members if they help you with your bags or offer extra services.

Tour guides: It's usual to tip your tour guide if you join one of their led excursions. Depending on the tour's duration and level of quality, the price can vary, but as a general rule, it should be between $5 and $10 for half-day tours and $10 to $20 for full-day excursions.

Taxi operators: Although it is not required in Kauai, it is customary to round up cab fares or add an extra 10% to 15% for excellent service.

Other services: It is typical to leave a gratuity of between 15% and 20% of the total bill for services like haircuts, massages, and spa visits.

Keep in mind that these are just suggestions; the decision to tip is ultimately yours. It's always good to express your gratitude with a larger tip if you receive great service.

Chapter 3:

Exploring Kauai Island

In this guide, we'll break down the island into four regions:

- South shore
- West shore
- East shore
- North shore

Here are the top twenty things to do before traveling to each shore:

- Take a boat tour or go on a trek along the magnificent Na Pali Coast, which is renowned for its high cliffs, verdant valleys, and amazing views.
- Discover the "Grand Canyon of the Pacific" in Waimea Canyon, which features colorful red and green cliffs, waterfalls, and expansive views.
- Hanalei Bay: Unwind on the stunning beach in the shape of a crescent, framed by verdant mountains and sprinkled with little beach communities.
- Explore the Kalalau Trail, which offers breathtaking views of the Na Pali Coast and hidden beaches, on a strenuous yet rewarding climb.
- Wailua River: Visit sights like Fern Grotto and Secret Falls by kayaking or taking a boat excursion along the lovely Wailua River.
- Poipu Beach: Take advantage of Poipu Beach's sunny shoreline, where you may swim, snorkel, surf, or just laze around.
- Explore the luxuriant and historically significant Limahuli Garden, which features native Hawaiian plants and offers stunning views of the North Shore.
- Visit Kauai Coffee Company to take a tour of the island's biggest coffee farm and discover how coffee beans are grown and roasted.
- Observe the Spouting Horn natural phenomenon, whereby strong waves send a stunning spray through a lava tube.

- Visit the quaint village of Hanapepe, which is renowned for its art galleries, old structures, and Friday Night Art Walk.
- Kilauea Lighthouse: Take in the stunning Kilauea Lighthouse, an iconic structure that provides sweeping views of the coastline and a chance for birdwatching.
- Visit Allerton Garden, a stunning botanical garden with exotic plants, water features, and sculptures, on a guided tour.
- Tunnels Beach: Scuba or snorkel at Tunnels Beach, which is well-known for its colorful coral reefs, tropical fish, and sporadic sightings of sea turtles.
- Visit Koke'e State Park to explore the varied ecosystems, stroll along the trails, stop at viewpoint sites, and learn about unusual plant and animal species.
- Smith's Tropical Paradise: Enjoy a classic Hawaiian luau with authentic food, live music, hula dancing, and fire performances at Smith's Tropical Paradise.
- Hanalei Valley Lookout: Visit this viewpoint to take in the view of the Hanalei Valley, taro fields, and flowing Hanalei River.
- Polihale State Park: Travel to Kauai's westernmost point and unwind on Polihale State Park's wide beach, which is renowned for its beautiful sunsets and golden beaches.
- Maha'ulepu Heritage Trail: Travel along the Maha'ulepu Heritage Trail for a beautiful coastal stroll as you pass

craggy cliffs, sand dunes, and historic Hawaiian monuments.

- The Kauai Museum, which offers exhibitions, artifacts, and educational activities, is a great place to learn about the island's past, present, and future.
- An exciting helicopter trip will give you a bird's-eye perspective of Kauai's breathtaking landscapes, including waterfalls, canyons, and secluded valleys.

Tourists' attraction sites and activities in each shore

South Shore

Makauwahi Cave

As one of Hawaii's largest limestone caverns, it is renowned for its cultural and scientific significance since it has revealed important details about the island's natural history and human occupancy.

The limestone in the area was eroded by freshwater and saltwater, among other geological processes, to create the cave. The main entrance opens into the "Great Room," a sizable chamber with a number of chambers and tunnels.

Archaeological digs in Makauwahi Cave have produced a plethora of artifacts and fossils that show past human activities and the ecological history of the island. Layers of silt that have collected over thousands of years are preserved in the cave, providing a unique record of environmental change.

Ancient stone tools, pottery shards, and plant remains have all been found at Makauwahi Cave and show that Native Hawaiian communities once existed there hundreds of years ago. The Kauai mole duck and the Kauai 'o'o are two extinct bird species whose fossils have been found in the cave.

With continued attempts to explore its geological and archaeological significance, Makauwahi Cave has emerged as a significant location for research and teaching. The cave is a component of the Makauwahi Cave Reserve, which also includes a limestone sinkhole and a system of coastal dunes, as well as a surrounding area with numerous different habitats.

Visitors can take guided tours of the reserve to explore the cave and learn about its significance for science and culture. It offers a rare chance to observe how closely people and the environment have interacted throughout Kauai's history.

To reach this fascinating spot, which is an active archeological site, follow the beach directions for Maha'ulepu Beaches. You must crouch down and enter a little rock tunnel even though the collapsed cave is open to the air. There won't be a chain barring the entrance in the field to your right if the cave is open to the public (just past the light blue shack). Daily 10–2 guided tours are available (or until 4 on Sunday). But keep in mind that this is Kauai, so don't make any firm plans. Maha'ulepu may be closed, yet it is still accessible.

Spouting Horn

This blowhole is a natural waterspout that is brought about by wave motion.

The Spouting Horn is located in the Poipu neighborhood of Kauai, next to Lawai Road and a short distance to the east of Poipu Beach Park. It has a designated parking lot and is easily reached by automobile.

Geological Formation: When ocean waves strike an undersea lava tube or tunnel, the spouting effect is produced. Water shoots up through a small opening as it rushes into the tube and pressure builds, creating a stunning spray of water and mist.

The attraction is situated in Spouting Horn Park, which has a gorgeous seaside scenery, restrooms, a grassy picnic area, and a few merchants selling trinkets and regional crafts. Visitors can take in the beautiful surroundings, observe the spouting activity, and explore the local tide pools.

Chanting and Legend: The Spouting Horn, according to Hawaiian tradition, is thought to be a mo'o, or a large lizard, that a local fisherman once captured inside the lava tube. The spout's loud hissing noise is thought to be the mo'o's roar. Locals frequently chant and blow conch shells, which adds to the site's ethereal atmosphere.

Safety Advice: Although the Spouting Horn is a magnificent sight, it is important to take precautions when going. The blowhole spray can be powerful, so it's best to maintain a safe distance and take a step back. To prevent any mishaps, stay away from the edge and stay off the rocks.

Visitors to the island should not miss the Kauai Spouting Horn, which offers a rare natural spectacle and a window into Hawaiian mythology. Respect the area, abide by any posted signs or instructions, and take in the breathtaking coastline scenery.

About a mile away, across from the Poipu roundabout, is the entrance to Allerton and McBryde Gardens. If you're already in the area, have a look. In addition, the region is home to several chicken families (birds, not people), as well as shops that sell commodities.

You can get a wonderful view of the water by continuing past Spouting Horn to the end of the road and turning around at the gate. Stop your car to the side and watch the spectacle. Native plants have been encouraged and restored in this area. In the spring, whales give birth to their calves close to this coast.

Turtles in Whaler's Cove

There is a considerable probability you will see turtles in the waters at Whaler's Cove when it comes to turtles. The coastal seas of Kauai are frequently home to the Hawaiian green sea turtle, or honu. Because of their placid disposition, people frequently encounter these turtles swimming close to the coast or sunbathing on sandy beaches.

It's crucial to keep in mind that sea turtles are protected by the Endangered Species Act and that it is forbidden to touch or otherwise harm them. In Whaler's Cove, if you come across a turtle while snorkeling or diving, it is recommended to keep your distance and respect its natural behavior.s

At the extreme left end of their parking lot, there are stairs that down to the cove. Disregard the trespassing signs. The cove is open to everyone; those signs are only for the uninitiated. Leave your automobile in the street if you're worried. In the fall and winter, sea turtles approach this little cove after dusk to rest. There are a lot of them (in the fall, and in November and December too). The hour or so before dusk is the best time to visit. If the surf and wind are particularly calm when they come up for air, you can hear them inhale. Magical.

If you intend to travel to Whaler's Cove or any other area where sea turtles are found, be sure to engage in responsible tourism and abide by local ordinances to safeguard these lovely animals and their habitat.

Kauai Coffee

You can take a self-guided tour of the coffee farm, learn how coffee is grown and processed, and taste a selection of their coffees.

The Kauai Coffee Estate, which offers tours of the plantation, is another place visitors to Kauai can go. From planting and harvesting through roasting and packaging, the trips give participants an understanding of the coffee-growing process. Both visitors and coffee connoisseurs enjoy visiting it.

Due to its dedication to environmentally friendly agricultural methods, Kauai Coffee has achieved notoriety. To lessen their influence on the environment, they use strategies including water conservation, recycling, and the use of renewable energy sources.

In general, Kauai Coffee is renowned for producing fine, flavorful coffee that highlights the distinctive features of the Kauai region.

They also have one of our favorite gift shops, which has both common and uncommon products.

Allerton and McBryde Gardens

This site is fantastic whether you are into plants or not. It is a portion of the National Tropical Botanical Garden and is located directly across from Spouting Horn at the end of Lawai Road from the Poipu roundabout.

Plants, flowers, trees, fruit, statues, and other things are there. All of the tour guides are very knowledgable and hospitable, but Sam is particularly exceptional.

Try their self-guided "Behind the Scenes" tour, which includes a trip to the plant nursery and a stroll to a pond in the top garden. However, there are frequently guides roaming the area who will give you an impromptu lecture. They are developing a part with traditional canoe plants and structures in this lovely location.

Before boarding the bus, stock up on bug juice in the waiting room.

Our suggestion for a great evening is the Allerton Sunset Tour. Make a reservation because it might not be available every day. You get to explore parts of the garden that aren't included in the standard tours, like the seashore and home of Allerton. Dinner is included in the excursion. Robert Allerton was a wealthy guy who loved art and nature, and he created and built the entire estate. His tale is really intriguing. The laws would not let him to leave his estate to the guy he loved and shared a home with. Robert thus took him in as his "son". That gap was immediately plugged by the authorities.

Advice: The Allerton trips are somewhat expensive. If it helps, your money helps them with their preservation and education efforts, and it might even be tax deductible (ask your bean counter). They frequently give discount codes if you book online at least one day in advance.

Ziplining with Outfitters Kauai

This zipline trip is enjoyable. Try the Adrenaline Tour, which features a high-speed zipline across the valley that you can ride prone like "Superman" and concludes with a short T-bar line into a swimming hole. The guides are extremely thorough and cautious while also using an odd mixture of smart-ass safety-related comedy. Instead of their Poipu round-about location,

Outfitter Kauai's tour departs from their Kipu Ranch facility on Kipu Road.

Recommendation: Check out ziplining at Princeville Ranch if you're up on the north coast.

Hyatt Hotel

You'll like making your way down to the beach through the lobby, which features exotic birds, a decent coffee shop, and lots of comfortable chairs. There are numerous lagunas for swimming, pathways, and seats to discover. Go picnicking! If you're cool about it and hide your non-Hyatt towels while swimming, the employees might assume you're staying there. If it helps, you can help them out by purchasing a $15 mai tai at the bar.

Tip: You can also park at Shipwreck Beach (see Beaches) and enter the Hyatt lagoon area by walking through the gate.

There is a waterslide, but in order to use it, you must have a hotel wristband.

Advice: Accents is a convenience store located immediately outside the lobby. The costs are oddly reasonable and it's nice and cool.

Kauai Humane Society – Dog Field Trip

Just west of Lihue on Highway 50 is a contemporary structure home to the Kauai Humane Society. They'll let you borrow one for a field trip in order to aid the socialization and adoption of their canines. You'll receive a towel, leash, snacks, and a cool "Adopt Me" vest (for the dog, not you). You can go on an expedition with the dog for an hour or all day. When meeting residents and other guests, mentioning that you have a dog is a terrific conversation starter.

Advice: Every day but Wednesday is acceptable for a field excursion.

West Shore

Waimea Hawaiian Church

Do you want to hear some serious spiritual hymn singing? This isn't for everyone. Visit the church in Hawaii. It begins at nine on Sunday. There will probably be nobody else from the mainland. You won't understand a word because the whole thing is in Hawaiian. You acquire chicken skin when they sing harmoniously while standing still (Hawaiian slang for goose bumps). Put some cash in the collection basket as a sign of aloha. The church is a white structure in Waimea and is located on the ocean side of the main road.

Most navigation systems are, for whatever reason, in stealth mode; if you discover Wrangler's Steakhouse or Big Save in Waimea, you're there.

Hanapepe Art Night

Every Friday from 5 to 9 p.m., "art night" is held in the tiny hamlet of Hanapepe. There are food trucks, street sellers, and music in addition to the fact that all the stores stay open late (well, 9 p.m. is late by Kauai standards). Several of the shops sell local artists' creations, many of whom are present to interact with customers. There's also a fantastic bookstore there (see Talk Story Bookstore). Enjoy Art Night and consider getting some jewelry or a tiny etching, but keep in mind that it's really understated and not for everyone.

Find the footbridge over the river (it's on the same side as Talk Story Bookstore, along a path between two buildings). It's kind of cool to stand there at night.

Combining Art Night and the west side Tasting Kauai tour is a good idea (see Activities). Just before Art Night starts, the tour ends at Hanapepe.

Talk Story Bookstore

Visit Talk Story in Hanapepe if you enjoy reading or even if you don't. They assert that they are the most western independent bookshop in the country; ideally, Kekaha won't get one. You can visit Talk Story whenever you choose, but you can also go to Hanapepe Art Night while you're there.

When you walk in, the store's owner, Ed Justus, would probably welcome you and offer to give you a tour. Say "yes"! Their assortment is eclectically and beautifully chosen, so you're sure to find something new there. They also give amusing gifts.

Helpful hint: The expression "talk story" is Hawaiian slang for "shoot the breeze" or idle chitchat. It does not imply spreading rumors or disparaging others because that is "talk stink." Being such a small island, Kauai is hardly the place to talk trash. That is a generally sound rule.

Tasting Kauai

This is a sampling tour that stops at various eateries and retail establishments, providing tasting samples and information at each stop. Numerous spots all throughout Kauai are where Tasting Kauai offers excursions. The only walking tour in Hanapepe is the West Shore tour; all other tours need you to get in your car and drive to the next destination.

You will enjoy the strolling because it will provide you some exercise in between courses and give you more opportunity to converse with your tour guide and other tourists. The enormous serving sizes at each stop will surprise you; they build up to a full lunch spread out over a few hours. In addition to talking to the restaurant and business owners, guides can provide information on the history of Hanapepe town.

Tasting Kauai provides a portion of its earnings to regional food banks on the island of Kauai. The cuisine is of the highest quality and is sourced locally whenever feasible.

On Friday, the West Shore tour concludes shortly before Hanapepe Art Night kicks out, allowing you to preserve your fantastic parking location and stick around for Talk Story Books and Art Night.

Kauai Kookie Factory Store

Although Kauai Kookies are sold in stores all over the island, if you visit the manufacturing facility in Hanapepe, you can find a wide variety of flavors and designs that aren't often available. Free samples are offered by them. If you enjoy sweets and are already passing through Hanapepe, it is worthwhile to stop in.

Despite the fact that it is the actual factory where they are created, only the retail store is open for excursions.

Salty Wahine

This small store is located in Hanapepe near to the Kauai Kookie Factory Store. Woman is pronounced "wah HEEN ay." They have a variety of salts and sugars with unique flavors that are manufactured in-house in the back of the store. You'll adore their hot lava on almost anything and their guava garlic salt on meat. Don't worry if you run out at home because you can get more from their website.

Refillable grinders are a smart idea, as you know. The grinding improves the spice's adhesion to food and increases its penetration.

Waimea Canyon

On the Hawaiian island of Kauai, there is a beautiful natural wonder called Waimea Canyon. It is frequently referred to as the "Grand Canyon of the Pacific" and is a well-liked vacation spot for those who enjoy the outdoors and the natural world.

The following are some significant Waimea Canyon facts:

Location: Waimea Canyon is located in Waimea Canyon State Park on the western side of Kauai. Waimea's town makes it simple to get there by automobile.

Geology and Formation: The Waimea River and the fall of the volcano that originally gave rise to Kauai eroded the canyon over the course of millions of years, forming it. The varied mineral deposits in the rocks are what give the canyon walls their vivid hues, which range from red to green.

Waimea Canyon is one mile (1.6 kilometers) wide, measures around 14 miles (22.5 kilometers) in length, and has a depth of

49

3,600 feet (1,100 meters). It is a magnificent sight due to its size and contrasting hues. The canyon's natural beauty is enhanced by its luxuriant foliage, waterfalls, and variety of flora and wildlife.

Trails and hiking: Waimea Canyon has a variety of trails for hikers of all levels of experience. The Canyon Trail, Cliff Trail, and Awaawapuhi Trail are a few of the well-known trails. These routes offer chances to discover the canyon's distinctive topography and take in expansive views of the surroundings.

Lookouts: Along State Highway 550, the main thoroughfare, there are a number of viewing sites that provide breathtaking views of the canyon. The Waimea Canyon Lookout, which offers a sweeping view of the canyon's vastness and the nearby Na Pali Coast, is the most well-known vantage point.

Weather: Because the weather in Waimea Canyon is unpredictable, it is best to be prepared. The canyon's higher elevations may be colder and wetter than its coastal regions. When organizing your visit, it's a good idea to look up the weather forecast and pack appropriately.

At some point during your journey, you have to make sure to drive up the Waimea Canyon and check out the views. If you can arrive at the final viewpoint (Pu'u o Kila) early in the day, your chances of seeing anything amazing will be higher. You can find yourself simply staring into a cloud bank later on in the day and wondering what the fuss is about.

The UKG suggests traveling up to Kekaha on the 550 from Waimea and returning by the Koke'e route (552). Following the major signs, it is recommended to continue along the coast past Waimea and then drive up into Kekaha. Then, as you make your way back, turn left onto 550 and descend into Waimea while taking in the spectacular views along the ridgeline.

Visitor advice: If you're going to Waimea Canyon, you should pack water, sunscreen, and insect repellent. It's also a good idea to wear sneakers or hiking boots that are comfortable. To protect the fragile ecosystem, keep to the pathways that have been established and respect the environment.

Overall, a trip to Waimea Canyon is a special experience that gives you the chance to take in Kauai's natural beauty and take in its breathtaking magnificence.

East Shore

Luau at Smith's Tropical Paradise

At Smith's Tropical Paradise in Wailua, try out a luau. It's located in a lovely garden area, and you can take a tram around for a narrated tour of the local flora and animals (including peacocks). The mai tais are weak but plentiful, and the food is standard all-you-can-eat luau fare. They'll enable you to completely enjoy the corny but frequently lovely dancing performance that follows dinner. Make a booking.

Advice: Long tables are used for family-style sitting. For groups of six or more, they will reserve spots; smaller groups must find their own seats.

To avoid eating poi alone, follow this advice. Into it, dip some kalua pork. Ono!

Grove Farm Museum Tour

This location is hidden away in Lihue, next to Safeway and Costco. You'd never guess that the area contains 100 acres of grounds and historic dwellings, including the original homes of the Wilcox family. A fascinating peek at the past and way of life of an early sugar plantation family may be found on the guided walking tour. In addition, they have a huge collection of documents, books, and artifacts that date back to the late 1970s, when the last member of the Wilcox family lived there.

.

A Hindu temple is being built by hand by craftsmen out of granite, however this is only briefly mentioned in UKG. Even after decades of work, they are still not finished. You can visit the lovely gardens at any time, but you must make a reservation by contacting 888-735-1619 in order to take the free tour and see the stone temple itself (because parking is so scarce). You will gain some knowledge about Hinduism and their endeavor. You must wear modestly; shawls are available for loan if necessary.

Douse yourself in bug repellant before entering. For whatever reason, those Hindu mosquitoes are very aggressive.

Coconut Coasters - Bike Rentals

The Coconut Coasters store is located on the ocean side at the northernmost part of Kapa'a. The trail has only slight inclines, the bikes are incredibly smooth and easy to peddle, and the coastal vistas are stunning when you ride in the direction of the north. Even a basket is available for carrying your belongings. The minimal amount of time is an hour, but if you want to explore both directions and make stops, allow two hours. Since there isn't much cover along the trail and the hot sun can burn you, you might want to pick the morning or afternoon.

You can earn a discount if you're sporting Seattle Seahawks apparel or if you successfully exclaim "Go Hawks!" to the merchant.

Kayaking on Wailua River

To get to the trailhead, you kayak up the (extremely calm) Wailua River. After that, you hike in to Secret Falls for lunch. a lot of fun.

They warn you not to stand beneath the falls because rocks could fall and hit you in the head. It's a lot of fun.

Koloa Rum Tasting

Need some free alcohol? (Well, a gram.) Visit the Koloa Rum Company at the Lihue-area Kilohana Plantation. They offer a great gift shop with loads of rum-related items, and you should check out their free rum tastings; just sign up at the counter. One of the remaining relics of the sugarcane plantation economy, their rum is produced from sugarcane cultivated on the island of Kauai. While visiting the plantation, you can stroll around the grounds, explore the iconic Gaylord's restaurant and bar, ride the extortionate train, or get some chocolate from the candy store.

Kauai Museum

The museum presents the past, present, and culture of Kauai and its inhabitants. Here are some details regarding the Kauai Museum:

Location: The Kauai Museum is located in the county seat of Kauai County, the town of Lihue. 4428 Rice Street, Lihue, Hawaii, 96766, is the address.

The museum's displays include a wide range of topics that reflect many facets of Kauai's history and culture. These include exhibits on prehistoric Hawaiian antiquities, traditional crafts, Captain James Cook's arrival, items from the plantation era, and the significance of sugar in Kauai's past. The displays provide information about the island's geological formation, early settlement, and indigenous people's traditions and customs.

Items: The Kauai Museum is home to a sizable collection of historical artifacts from Kauai. These include vintage household goods, weapons, and equipment utilized by the Native Hawaiians. The museum also features old pictures, pieces of art, and records that add more background information on the island's past.

Activities & Programs: To engage visitors and foster an awareness of Kauai's culture, the museum sponsors a number of events and programs. There may be storytelling sessions, cultural demonstrations, educational workshops, and performances of traditional music and dance among them.

Gift Store: The Kauai Museum features a gift shop where customers can buy a variety of goods, including books on Hawaiian history and culture, locally produced art, jewelry, and other Kauai-related souvenirs.

The museum is typically open Monday through Saturday from 9:00 am to 4:00 pm (hours are subject to change, so it's best to check the official website or call the museum for the most up-to-date information). There can be admission costs, and seniors, kids, and students might be eligible for discounts. The museum's website or direct contact is advised for the most recent details on opening times, admission costs, and any upcoming special events.

It is much better because your entrance fee includes a week-long pass and there are free docent presentations available a couple days a week at 10:30am.

Tubing in Irrigation Tunnels

You may go tubing through historic irrigation canals and tunnels in the interior of Kauai with Kauai Backcountry Adventures in Lihue. Although the UKG doesn't find it particularly enjoyable, you will. The active and entertaining young guides will share information about Kauai with you while you journey in the van and when you are out on the trail and canals. Through the tunnels, the water may move rather quickly, making for an exciting ride as you spin and bounce off the walls. Although the price is a little high, we would go on this unique excursion again with friends despite the price.

The guides advised against using insect repellent because the water is rushing so quickly. When the van stops at the valley lookout or before making your way down the trail to the launch point, you should rub some bug juice on your skin, particularly your ankles.

North Shore

Kilauea Lighthouse

You can observe the birds soaring on the breeze and stare down to the lake and lighthouse peninsula from the road. But if you want the complete experience, we suggest spending the ten dollars and making the short trek to the lighthouse. There is a lot of information about the history of the lighthouse, including a video of a guide demonstrating the various features of the building and revolving light mechanism. While you cannot enter the historic building (except on a guided tour on Wednesdays and Saturdays), you can view it from the outside. The little shop there has some nice books and mementos, including a paper map - Kaua'i Island Atlas and Maps by Robert Seimer. The views along the route are breathtaking.

Ziplining at Princeville Ranch

Visit Princeville Ranch Adventures today. There are several possibilities available to them; they ought to select the one that includes lunch at a swimming hole. For Kauai Ono, they pitched the tent in their front yard.

Other excursions and outdoor activities are available at Princeville Ranch, allowing guests to discover and take in Kauai's natural splendor. The ranch also provides other well-liked activities, some of which are:

1. Riding a horse: Visitors can take guided horseback riding tours to explore the ranch's gorgeous paths and take in the tranquil environment of the surrounding area.
2. Hiking & Nature Walks: Princeville Ranch offers a number of hiking and nature paths that lead tourists through stunning natural settings, such as valleys, streams, and tropical forests. These escorted hikes offer the chance to discover the island's history, flora, and fauna.
3. Kayaking & Stand-Up Paddleboarding: The ranch provides guided kayaking and stand-up paddleboarding tours on the Hanalei River so that guests can explore the waterways and take in the peace and quiet of the area.
4. Princeville Ranch offers guided trips to the exclusive waterfalls on their property. Visitors can enjoy the spectacular cascades surrounded by lush foliage while taking a relaxing plunge in the natural pools.

The ranch emphasizes environmentally friendly procedures and encourages environmental preservation. It provides a variety of activities ideal for families, couples, and outdoor lovers seeking to commune with nature and discover Kauai's natural beauty.

Sunset Golf Cart Tour at Makai Golf Club

In essence, you arrive a few hours before dusk. The tracking system is Kauai-casual, so you need contact beforehand (808.826.1912) to get your name on the list. They appeared surprised to see us both times. While you wait to go, enjoy a shockingly inexpensive happy hour at the cantina. A golf professional will accompany you on the course while sharing tales, pointing out plants, animals, and breathtaking scenery.

Take bug juice since mosquitoes might become active as the sun sets.

Advice: You have a good chance of seeing nesting albatross parents or chicks up close if you go in the winter or spring.

Na 'Aina Kai Botanical Gardens

It is a private garden with a spectacular display of tropical plants, flowers, and landscapes spread across more than 240 acres of land.

The garden was built by Joyce and Ed Doty with the intention of preserving and sharing Kauai's natural beauty. A formal garden, a children's garden, a hardwood plantation, a moss and fern garden, a meadow, and a desert garden are just a few of the themed gardens that can be found at Na ina Kai, which translates to "Lands by the Sea" in Hawaiian.

Visitors at Naina Kai have the option of taking guided or unguided walks through the grounds. While the self-guided walks let tourists explore at their own pace, the guided tours give detailed information on the many species and sceneries. Special activities at the garden include art exhibitions, music, and educational programs.

The Sculpture Park, which houses a collection of more than 80 contemporary sculptures by renowned artists, is one of the centerpieces of Na Ina Kai Botanical Gardens. The natural surroundings of the garden are incorporated into these sculptures, resulting in a distinctive and engrossing experience.

Naina Kai also includes a lovely beachside area called "Sunset Point" in addition to the gardens. Weddings and other special events are frequently held in this region because of the breathtaking ocean vistas it affords.

But if you're staying in the north, this autonomous, nonprofit garden is extremely cool, and it's in a good spot. A guided tram tour makes stops along the way where you can get out and go for a short walk. The sculptures are amazing, and the native and invading plant species are discussed in an interesting way.

In general, Kauai's Na 'ina Kai Botanical Gardens should not be missed by nature lovers and those looking for a tranquil, enchanted setting.

Limahuli Garden

This is the third National Tropical Botanical Garden on the island of Kauai, following Allerton and McBryde Gardens on the south shore. It is located close to the end of the road on the north coast, before Ke'e Beach.

The conservation and preservation of native Hawaiian plants and ecosystems is a priority at Limahuli Garden and Preserve. It displays a wide variety of plants, including endangered and unusual species that can only be found in Hawaii. Each section of the garden represents a different Hawaiian habitat, such as a coastal, lowland, upland, or montane ecosystem.

Visitors to Limahuli Garden can stroll along the garden's trails and take in the surrounding natural splendor. The routes provide expansive views of the ocean and mountains while passing through tropical forests and over streams. Additionally, the garden offers educational activities and interpretive displays to teach visitors about local flora, customs, and the value of conservation.

This gorgeous valley is home to a wide variety of carefully maintained flora, some of which are endangered. We strongly suggest joining a guided tour. You'll learn so much more about the flora, the history of the island, the garden, and even a few Hawaiian stories for only $40 as opposed to $20. Get your drink on because there might be mosquitos in certain gloomy areas if the wind isn't blowing. Because it rains more frequently on the north coast, it's a good idea to bring an umbrella or hat. You'll easily dry off when the sun comes out again.

Advice: At 10:00 am, the escorted trips start. Depending on where you're staying, the trip requires a major time commitment because driving from Poipu will take at least 90 minutes. Do it!

Beaches

Prepare yourself beforehand for a relaxing vacation of snorkeling and relaxation. Snorkeling equipment can be rented by the week; simply store it in the trunk of your car to keep it available at all times. Even though you can rent equipment almost anyplace, Snorkel Bob's and Seasport Divers are reliable options. Check to see if the property has beach chairs if you are staying there (check the closet). Rent them if not, then leave them in the car! At Seasport Divers near the Poipu roundabout, there are chairs in the Tommy Bahama design that resemble backpacks. We're telling you, having chairs at the beach will make you happy.

Advice: Avoid attempting to walk while wearing fins; you risk falling and will undoubtedly be recognized as a tourist. Put your mask on first before wading out into the water while holding your fins in a sandy area until you are about waist deep. Get into the water between waves while breathing through your snorkel, then don your fins. Reverse the procedure to return to land when you're ready. When the water is shallow enough, swim until it, then kneel to take off your fins before leaving.

Keep one eye on the ocean when you're at the beach or on the rocks. You can be caught off guard by a large wave and fall. When a wave approaches when you are in the water, pivot and stand with your legs apart sideways to the wave. The likelihood of you remaining upright will be higher.

Almost every beach on Kauai might have a monk seal lazing around. At Salt Ponds, Poipu, and Beach House/Lawai Road, you can see them. It is forbidden to interfere with them in any manner since they are endangered. A rope barrier will be erected around a monk seal by a volunteer monk seal response team to warn tourists to keep their distance.

Remember that seals need a clear path to safety and advise against walking on the beach or in the shallow areas between them and the water.

There are a ton of beaches on Kauai, and UKG provides excellent descriptions. Here are a handful of the most popular ones, along with some helpful information.

South Shore

Maha'ulepu Beaches

- Lounging
- Walking
- Seclusion

Although there are several distinct beaches along this area, we just refer to it as Maha'ulepu. Let's talk about how to pronounce "mah HA leh poo." You may have a favorite beach that you frequently visit called Kawailoa Bay. It's wonderful for relaxing, reading, strolling, and shallow wading, but avoid swimming out because there isn't a reef to provide protection. There aren't any restrooms available. Here, because of their proximity to the water, the trees provide some nice shade. Kawailoa Bay doesn't see a lot of people, so you can have a stretch of the beach to yourself, especially during the workweek. There is also a fantastic trek that begins there; see Hikes and Walks.

The route to Maha'ulepu can be unsteady, but if you drive carefully and avoid the biggest potholes, your rental car should be alright. On this particular route, you'll be happy you leased an SUV. (Once the road in Poipu turns to gravel, continue past the Hyatt. After CJM Stables, turn a couple times (the alternatives will be gated closed). You will eventually arrive at a parking space with a puddle in the center. It's Gillin's Beach here. But don't stop there; continue on the dirt road to the left until it ends at Kauailoa Bay, where there are additional parking spaces. Since the gates are locked at sunset, leave before 6 o'clock.

You will directly pass the guard shack designating the field leading to Makauwahi Cave on the rough road to Maha'ulepu.

Advice: Grove Farms, the company that owns the road that leads to Maha'ulepu, occasionally closes the road for upkeep (or for movie filming.) You can see if the road is closed as mentioned on the Makauwahi Cave website. In any case, if the road is gated, you can park at CJM Stables and enter on foot, or you can wait until a different day. The cave may be reached in approximately 10 minutes, and Kawailoa Bay in another 20. Con: entering with all of your belongings. Even greater privacy is a plus.

Beach House/Lawai Road

- Snorkeling
- Lounging
- Sunset

Just a few minutes from the Poipu roundabout, Lawai Road Beach is located alongside the road to Spouting Horn. Right in front of the Beach House restaurant is a little sandy beach. There is typically excellent snorkeling there, particularly in the winter and early in the day when the ocean is calmer. Despite the fact that "Lawai Beach" is actually a different beach in Allerton Garden, some people still refer to it as such.

Koloa Landing

- Snorkeling
- Scuba Diving

Whaler's Cove is a rocky cove with a boat ramp that is well-liked by snorkelers and divers but is not a beach. Just south of the Poipu roundabout, on Hoonani Road, is where you may locate it. The quantity of runoff from the nearby Waikomo Stream and the swell pouring in from the south determine the visibility, which is erratic. Before diving in, you can inspect it by strolling along the rocky wall that surrounds the cove and taking a look at the sea below. The water is rather clear if you can see the rocky bottom (polarized sunglasses are helpful here). There are several fish and sea turtles to view when the conditions are ideal.

Baby Beach

- Lounging
- Sunsets (especially winter)

This is a little neighborhood beach close to the Poipu roundabout. It's only useful for relaxing, reading, and enjoying a beverage while watching the sunset. Oh, those sound like some fun things to do! From Lawai Road, turn into Hoona Road, and follow the route between two homes to the beach. On Kauai, beaches are open to the public, and there are tucked-away access paths all around the island. Although they might not have signs, it is quite acceptable to use them. Local keiki (children) frequently play in the small lagoon during the week. In the winter, when the sun is still lowering into the lake, the sunsets here are very spectacular (in April it reaches the land). Visitors and locals alike will frequently introduce themselves to you as they congregate to have drinks while watching the entertainment. You will only ever see the green flash here.

Sheraton Beach

- Swimming
- Lounging
- Boogie boarding

The Poipu Sheraton boasts lovely gardens that are right next to the ocean. You can bring own chairs and sit along the beach, or you can find a grassy spot under the palm trees at the Sheraton or a rocking chair there. On the roadside closest to the ocean, there are public parking areas on both ends of the hotel complex.

Tip: Locate the grassy area with fire pits immediately outside RumFire. In the rockers, it's a nice place to unwind. The breeze sweeps right through, even on the warmest summer days.

Poipu Beach

- Lounging
- Sunset
- Swimming
- Snorkeling
- Lifeguard

The epitome of a Kauai beach is Poipu Beach. There are plenty of sandy beaches for relaxing and people-watching, a sheltered little lagoon for swimming, and a fantastic snorkeling spot. Yes, it is a well-known beach, but there is usually parking and a small patch of sand available. The tombolo, a stretch of sand that extends to a rocky area, is what makes Poipu Beach unique. Sometimes you may stand in the middle of the beach and have water gently lapping at your feet from both sides because the waves come in from both directions. Tombolos are extremely rare; there are reportedly just three in the entire Hawaiian archipelago, all on Kauai, and Poipu is the only one that can be reached.

The tombolo has been eroding in recent years due to storm surges, but normal wave movement ought to be putting it back together.

Brenneke's Beach

- Boogie boarding
- Lounging

Brenneke's Beach is located over to the left across the grassy area (facing the water) from Poipu Beach. Many folks come here to boogie board. It's simple to attempt boogie boarding; after checking your condo's closet, head across the street to Nukumoi to rent the necessary equipment (a board and short flippers). Simply ensure that there are many others in the water, preferably some locals. There may be a reason why you're the only person present; the situation could be hazardous. Don't ride too far in near the shore at Brenneke's, especially where the rocks are.

Tip: Kick your fins to start moving in the same direction as the wave as it approaches you from behind. Push the front of the board down with your arms as the wave approaches you to begin sliding down the wave's "slope."

Shipwreck Beach

- Lounging
- Boogie boarding

The Hyatt Hotel is directly near to this vast, sandy beach. There, the wave movement can be very strong. Crazy people jump into the lake from a rocky point on the left.

West Side

Salt Ponds Beach Park

- Swimming
- Lounging
- Lifeguard

There is lots of space for relaxing in this attractive park, which also has a wonderful sandy beach. Although the water is safe for swimming, it is frequently too murky for decent snorkeling. There is a higher than usual likelihood of spotting a monk seal.

Polihale Beach

- Seclusion
- Sunset
- Big waves

Although some people mistakenly believe that Polihale means "home of the afterlife," it simply refers to the place where people's spirits pass on. There are not many people on the long, empty beach. We were once given the advice to "move a mile farther down" if Polihale became too crowded by a local. This is a terrific spot to relax, take in the sunset while sipping a drink or eating a picnic dinner, and watch the surf crash onto the sand. Except for shallow wading in the waves, it is not a nice area to be in the water. Watch the surf with one eye.

Investment is required to get there. To reach the beaches, you must first travel 5 miles on a very bumpy, pothole-filled road to the island's far west end along the south shore. UKG has clear instructions. There are numerous cautionary warnings, but if the road appears to be safe (i.e., dry enough), proceed cautiously and slowly. Driving to Polihale is frowned upon by rental car companies, but if you're feeling adventurous, it's a terrific trip.

Drive to the west coast of Kauai if you need some sun because it seems to be raining everywhere else. The driest parts of Kauai are located in the westernmost regions, including Polihale.

North Shore

Ke'e Beach

- Lounging
- Sunset (especially summer)
- Snorkeling
- Hiking

"Keh AY" when spoken. This is one of Kauai's most beautiful sunset locations, but getting there requires a drive, especially from the south shore. The physical end of the road is past Hanalei. Due to the presence of a protected reef, snorkeling is excellent here when the circumstances are favorable, especially during the summer. Here is also where the Kalalau Trail along the Na Pali coast begins.

Hideaways

- Lounging
- Seclusion
- Swimming

Hideaways is a fantastic beach that few people will visit if they're not eager for a challenging (though brief) hike. It is in the Princeville region; UKG provides clear directions. Winters can be rough on the lake, so be cautious before entering.

Chapter 4:

Itineraries

3 Days Itinerary

Day 1:

1. Morning: Visit Waimea Canyon State Park to kick off your day. This magnificent natural wonder, also referred to as the "Grand Canyon of the Pacific," provides beautiful views and a variety of hiking trails. Explore the park for a while, soaking in the expansive views.

2. Afternoon: Travel to Hanapepe, a town renowned for its quaint art galleries, shops, and plantation-style structures. Visit Hanapepe Swinging Bridge and enjoy a leisurely

stroll around the neighborhood's streets and local art galleries.

3. Evening: Take a drive to Polihale State Park to watch the sunset on Kauai's west side. Large lengths of this remote beach's golden sand and breathtaking views have made it famous. Enjoy a picnic meal while admiring the magnificent ocean sunset.

Day 2:

1. Early in the morning, set off on a boat tour of the Na Pali Coast. The spectacular cliffs, sea caves, and crystal-clear turquoise waters that make up this famous coastline are well known. Choose a sailing or snorkeling cruise to discover the abundant marine life and breathtaking coastal vistas.

2. Afternoon: Travel to the picturesque community of Kapa'a on Kauai's eastern shore. Explore the quaint streets that are home to many independent stores, boutiques, and eateries. The Kapa'a Bike Path, a beautiful track that parallels the beach, should not be missed.

3. Visit the Wailua Falls in the evening; it is a magnificent 80-foot waterfall close to Lihue. Enjoy the stunning scenery and take some pictures. For a more immersive experience, you can also climb to the neighboring Secret Falls (Uluwehi Falls) if time allows.

Day 3:

Early in the morning, begin your day by touring the North Shore. Start by going to Hanalei Bay, a stunning beach with a crescent shape where you can swim and unwind. The Hanalei River can also be explored by renting a kayak or paddleboard.

Drive to the nearby town of Princeville in the afternoon to play a round of golf at the illustrious Princeville Makai Golf Club. This championship course provides breathtaking ocean vistas along with an enjoyable round of golf.

Evening: Take a dinner cruise along the coast as the sun sets to cap off your vacation in Kauai. Sail along the stunning shoreline while enjoying a fantastic supper and watching the sun set.

Please take note that this itinerary gives you a broad idea of how to spend your three days in Kauai. Prior to your visit, be careful to check for any closures, weather alerts, or availability of a particular tour.

6 Days itinerary

Day 1:

1. Morning: Go on a hike to Hanakapiai Falls to start the day. The hike is roughly 8 kilometers round trip and has a trailhead at Ke'e Beach. It leads you past verdant

rainforests, over streams, and eventually to a magnificent waterfall.

2. After the hike, unwind at Ke'e Beach's sandy shore. This is a wonderful location to unwind and enjoy the Na Pali Coast's natural beauty.

3. Evening: Have dinner in the adjacent village of Hanalei. Hanalei is a lovely town with lots of excellent eateries, cafes, and stores.

Day 2:

1. Early in the morning, fly above Kauai. The Waimea Canyon, Na Pali Coast, and waterfalls can all be seen in this amazing aerial view of the island.

2. After the helicopter tour, spend the day strolling along the Koloa Heritage Trail. The historical village of Koloa, which was once a thriving sugar plantation town, is being explored on foot during this tour. You'll pass by historic structures, churches, and famous sites along the walk.

3. Evening: Dine at Poipu, an upscale resort community on the island's southern tip. Poipu is an excellent area to watch a sunset and offers a lot of fantastic eateries.

Day 3:

1. Early in the morning, go snorkeling around the Na Pali Coast. This is a fantastic way to view the area's vibrant marine life.

2. Afternoon: Visit the Kauai Coffee Company after the snorkeling excursion. There are tours, tastings, and a gift store available at this coffee estate.
3. Evening: Enjoy dinner in Kapaa, a quaint town on the island's east coast. There are many fantastic restaurants and businesses in Kapaa, and it's a terrific spot to see live music.

Day 4:

1. Visit Waimea Canyon State Park in the morning. This park, also referred to as the "Grand Canyon of the Pacific," provides breathtaking views of the canyon and its surroundings.
2. After exploring the canyon, spend the afternoon in Lihue at the Kauai Museum. The museum features displays on the history, culture, and artwork of Hawaii.
3. Evening: Eat dinner at a restaurant or food truck nearby. On Kauai, there are lots of fantastic local eateries and food trucks serving real Hawaiian food.

Day 5:

1. Take a boat tour of the Na Pali Coast in the morning. You might even spot some dolphins or whales, and it's a terrific chance to explore the shoreline from a different angle.

2. After the boat excursion, spend the afternoon lounging on Hanalei Bay's beach. A stunning beach with a crescent shape, Hanalei Bay is perfect for swimming, surfing, or simply lounging in the sun.
3. Evening: Enjoy dinner and a live musical performance in Hanalei. In the evenings, a lot of the restaurants in Hanalei have live musical performances.

Day 6:

1. Visit the Limahuli Garden and Preserve in the morning. This botanical garden gives visitors a look at the native plants and historical culture of Kauai.
2. After touring the garden, head to Kilauea's northern shore in the afternoon. There are numerous fantastic stores, cafes, and galleries in this lovely town.
3. In the evening, eat dinner in Kapaa. There are several excellent restaurants in Kapaa, and it's a terrific spot to see live music.

Here's a suggested two-week itinerary for exploring the beautiful island of Kauai in Hawaii:

- Day 1: Arrival and unwinding
- After landing at Lihue Airport, take a taxi to your lodging.

- Spend the day unwinding, relaxing, and exploring the neighborhood beaches.

Day 2: North Shore Exploration

- Visit the quaint town of Hanalei on the North Shore.
- Take a day trip to Hanalei Bay, go snorkeling, or just relax on the beach.
- To see breathtaking views of the taro fields and mountains, go to the Hanalei Valley Lookout.

Day 3: Na Pali Coast Adventure

- Take a boat tour or helicopter ride to experience the breathtaking Na Pali Coast.
- Explore sea caves, admire towering cliffs, and keep an eye out for dolphins and whales.

Day 4: Waimea Canyon and Koke'e State Park

- See the "Grand Canyon of the Pacific" at Waimea Canyon.
- Enjoy the stunning views of the canyon and the lush woodlands on the hiking paths in Koke'e State Park.

Day 5: East Side Exploration

- Discover the East Side's natural splendor, which includes Opaekaa Falls and Wailua River State Park.

- Take an excursion in a boat or kayak to see the well-known Fern Grotto.

Day 6: Beach Day and Snorkeling

- Poipu Beach Park, renowned for its crystal-clear seas and excellent snorkeling, is a terrific place to unwind.
- Investigate the adjacent Spouting Horn, a blowhole where water is shot into the air.

Day 7: Hanapepe and South Shore

- Visit the lovely village of Hanapepe, which is renowned for its museums and historical structures.
- Discover the south shore's Lawai Beach and Shipwreck Beach.

Day 8: Waterfall Exploration

- Visit the breathtaking Wailua Falls, a two-tiered waterfall.
- Hike along Wailua River State Park to the Secret Falls or Uluwehi Falls.

Day 9: Relaxation and Local Culture

- Spend a relaxing day at the beach or treat yourself to a spa treatment.
- Attend a traditional Hawaiian luau in the evening to fully experience the culture of the region.

Day 10: Nāpali Coast State Wilderness Park

- Walk the Kalalau Trail in the Npali Coast State Wilderness Park, a strenuous hike.
- Admire the pristine beauty of the coastline and find undiscovered beaches.

Day 11: Kayaking and Snorkeling

- Go on a guided kayak excursion down the Wailua River to see waterfalls and lush surroundings.
- Visit Lydgate Beach Park and snorkel to see the vibrant marine life.

Day 12: Explore the Coconut Coast

- Start your exploration of the Coconut Coast by going to the Kauai Museum.
- Visit Kealia Beach and Donkey Beach while enjoying a picturesque drive along the coast.

Day 13: Hanalei Valley and Beaches

- Visit the Hanalei Valley on your way back to the North Shore for breathtaking vistas.
- Spend the day exploring the North Shore's beautiful beaches, including Tunnels Beach and Lumahai Beach.

Day 14: Departure

Take advantage of your last day in Kauai by lounging on the beach or shopping for last-minute souvenirs.

Depart from Lihue Airport and bid the lovely island of Kauai adieu.

Before your journey, don't forget to verify the local laws, the weather, and the accessibility of attractions since these can change.

Chapter 5:
Cuisine in Kauai

Fish tacos at Coconut Coast Lava Lava Beach Club

Your taste buds will undoubtedly be in for a treat when you eat a taco shell stuffed with tempura Mahi Mahi, salsa Fresca, coconut slaw, and wasabi aioli.

Pork Tenderloin at Kilohana's Gaylord's

With mushroom relish, wild rice, steaming bok choy, and Wi demi-glaze, a Hawaiian fruit, the pork tenderloin is baked and seasoned with Hawaiian chili peppers.

Hemingway Classic Fondue Art Cafe

This bubbling bowl of white wine coupled with smooth cheeses is served over a fire and is best shared with friends and family. It comes with a side dish of sliced sausage, apple, baked bread, and other pleasures for dipping.

Scallops with Crab Crusted Eating House 1849

This vibrant sea food dish is served over a rich bed of smoked unagi cream sauce and is topped with the chef's interpretation of sushi rice musubi.

The Sheraton Kauai Resort's Rum Fire Fried Brussels Sprouts

When mixed with Portuguese sausage, spiced macadamia almonds, and miso vinaigrette, these salty cruciferous veggies are bursting with flavor and protein.

Bowl of Nola Poi, Fresh Bite

The staple of the traditional Hawaiian diet is poi, a starchy, purple paste made from mashed taro root.

In this version of the traditional meal, coconut milk transforms the dish's traditionally sour flavor into a sinfully sweet pleasure. Similar to an acai bowl, this dish is topped with homemade granola and fresh fruit.

Hanalei Dolphin with Rainbow Poke Martini

This rainbow poke meal combines premium pieces of tuna, salmon, white fish, and avocado. It is served over sweet sushi rice with a generous spray of the chef's unique "Broke Da Mouth" sauce.

The Ahi Poke Nachos Nanea restaurant and bar are situated at the Westin Princeville Ocean Resort Villas.

A raw fish salad called ahi poke is so popular in Hawaii that it may be compared to having a cheeseburger there.

In this rendition of a local classic, the raw squares of fresh tuna are layered over a bed of crunchy nacho chips, giving it the Hawaiian flavor that has made it a fan favorite at Nanea Restaurant.

Kauai Kombucha Float Eat Healthily

What could be unpleasant about consuming locally made ginger-berry kombucha that has been dipped in homemade mixed happy ice cream? Both your palate and your digestive system will like this probiotic punch.

La Spezia's Nonna's Lasagna

This family recipe stacks lasagna noodles with four pieces of cheese, spinach, zucchini, and bechamel over your choice of bolognese or spicy arrabbiata sauce.

Ishihara Poke Bowl Market

The tastiest poke on the island is served at Ishihara Market, a mom-and-pop store founded in 1934 by Japanese immigrants, according to any local.

The Saimin of Saimin Hamura

The tastiest poke on the island is served at Ishihara Market, a mom-and-pop store founded in 1934 by Japanese immigrants, according to any local.

Chicken Wings at Happy Talk Lounge

Because they are made with a scorching hot yet delectable chocolate habanero sauce from Kauai Juice Co., these wings are a spicy food lover's dream.

The Local's Pork Belly Braised in Koloa Rum

To improve this meal of pork belly, flavors of the regional rum, jicama, pineapple, and pickled mustard seeds are added. Everything combines to provide a distinctive cuisine.

Cafe Loco Moco Anuenue

Loco Moco is arguably the best island-style breakfast. The Anuenue Cafe serves the neighborhood favorite with a spread of Kauai ground beef, rice, two eggs, and Kauai-grown mushrooms as well as a lot of homemade gravy.

Jerk Ragout Oasis on the Beach in Hanalei

This Kauai meal of ground buffalo meat is served with the traditional Jamaican flatbread, cassava bammy, and achiote-scented rice.

Acai Bowl Kalalea Juice Hale: The Next Level

This velvety mixture of Tambor acai—a Hanalei-based acai producer—banana, kale, protein powder, and fresh coconut milk is topped with handmade granola, banana slices, fresh coconut meat, honey, bee pollen, swirls of peanut butter, and a kale leaf.

Salmon Lomi Lomi

In this typical side dish, raw salmon is massaged (lomilomi) with salt, onions, and sometimes child before being served with tomatoes.

Poi

The main ingredient in Kauai's traditional dish, poi, is cooked, pounded taro that has been mixed with water and allowed to ferment. Its consistency might range from thick to runnier. Other options for eating poi can be found at the food trucks.

Chapter 6:
Affordable places to eat in Kauai.

If preparing and eating cup noodles every day for the remainder of your trip is not your style, there are several (relatively) more affordable options that many residents and thrifty travelers adore. As of October 2014, the following businesses were still operating and were well-liked for their ability to fill you up for less than $20 per person.

1) Tahiti Nui Hanalei Restaurant & Bar

Tahiti Nui, which was established in 1963 and is still run by the same family, is well-known in the area. This fusion eatery focuses on Hawaiian, Thai, and Italian cuisine. They take pride in their delicious seafood, relaxed ambience with outside dining, and very old but endearing Tiki bar decor, which is located just beside the Hanalei Pier on Kuhio Highway.

2) Kilauea Fish Market

This extremely unassuming, one-story, spotlessly clean shack with outside seating is situated at the end of Kilauea Road and serves delicious, fresh fish. The house-made teriyaki sauce and sesame island dressing are this restaurant's specialty, and while different guests have raved about diverse items, many claim they are addicting.

3) Kilauea Bakery & Pau Hana Pizza

It appears to be a house with indoor and outdoor eating, complete with a balcony where you can sit on stools, and is situated in the interior plaza of a small shopping complex. There are other strange signs and artifacts, such as a smaller, less expensive TGIF. Additionally, they provide a few gluten-free options, and if a whole pizza is too much for you, you can purchase it by the slice. A normal lunch offer will run you roughly $10 per person, including a drink and dessert.

4) Duane's Ono-Char Burger

It's actually a one-story, red and white-painted structure that is a hole in the wall. This is a typical roadside mom-and-pop business, complete with outside seating (but no restroom) and the yard's infamous wild chickens. Even though it only started doing business in the 1970s, the locals have come to love this establishment.

5) Monico's Taqueira

This one is undoubtedly a lot more posh despite the wooden outside benches. The restaurant's owner and chef, Monico Hernandez, is an East Los Angeles native. Although Tex-Mex is his specialty, several of his dishes have an Asian influence, like the fried spring rolls served with guacamole dip. Although the cost of the food is affordable, you'll need more money for the drinks.

6) Hukilau Lanai

This is unquestionably more upmarket and is situated beside its own poolside at the Kauai Coast Resort in Kapaa. Fortunately, their deals and several of their appetizers are around $20. Wine aficionados can choose from a large variety of bottles for under $20, but if you simply want a glass with your dinner, prices range from $5.75 to $6.

7) Kaua'i Community College

Head over to the college during the academic year if you want to experience exquisite dining without breaking the bank. Their Culinary Arts Program offers lunch daily from 10 am to 1 pm, but if you'd rather something fancier, they also provide fine dining.

For $17.50, a typical three-course menu prepared to Cordon Bleu standards includes an appetizer, an entree, and a dessert. Since students prepare and serve the food, you are required to fill out a remark card following your meal. However, you must contact in advance and make a reservation for this choice.

8) Hamura's Saimin Stand

This one stands out. Hamura's, which first opened for business in 1951, is another institution that has stayed in that time period. Due to the food, this unpretentious (and unclean) restaurant is where locals mingle with politicians and celebrities. Thankfully, the presence of such dignified clients has not affected their costs.

The state dish of Hawaii is saimin, which is noodle soup in the Hawaiian culture. America brought in a lot of Asians in the 1950s to work on Hawaii's thriving plantations, and many of them stayed. This meal still evokes the past and memories of those early settlers.

It is created with soft wheat egg noodles and served with hot sauce, green onions, Spam, and some Asian and local seasonings. The meal is difficult to identify because it incorporates elements of almost every culture that still exists on the islands today. Quintessentially Hawaiian, it is fully a mashup of Filipino pansit, Chinese mein, and Japanese ramen.

Hamura's is an official historic site of significance since it helped create this dish. It was recognized as one of America's Classics by the James Beard Foundation, a culinary organization, in 2006.

9) Lihue Barbecue Inn

This establishment is a bit more upscale and, despite its name, does not, for some reason, provide barbeque. As of 2014, it has been operating for 74 years and offers very sizable portions. They specialize in serving Hawaiian and Japanese cuisine, along with salads and delectable sweets.

10) Mark's Place

This difficult-to-find spot, which is not typically on the tourist map and is situated in an industrial park, mostly serves construction workers and knowledgeable locals. Although prices are modest, portions are large. Since the restaurant is designed for take-out, there isn't much space inside, but if you'd prefer to eat there, there are picnic tables outside that have umbrellas.

11) Keoki's Paradise

Some of their dishes are surprisingly affordable considering the opulent decor and atmosphere (imagine a Las Vegas take on the Hawaiian cliché, complete with burning torches). Aside from fresh seafood, they provide a wide range of things, although they don't really have any local specialties.

12) Sheraton Kauai Point

There are three restaurants at this hotel, each with a bar, and one cafe. Avoid RumFire's if you're on a tight budget because it charges more for its breathtaking 180o panoramic view of the beach. Although the costs for alcohol are somewhat high, Lava's on Poipu Beach is more affordable.

Go to Auli'i Lu'au if you want to spend some money and experience a Hawaiian luau with hula dancing. The cost of the all-you-can-eat buffet is $99.75 per person. Refills on drinks, including certain alcoholic ones, are included in that cost.

13) Sueoka's Store and Snack Shop

The inhabitants of Koloa visit this establishment, which has been there for at least 90 years, to buy their goods. If you're looking for a meal, a burger can cost $1.95, while a plate lunch consisting of pork or fish with rice and macaroni salad can run you around $6.50. There isn't any indoor or outdoor seating, but who cares when their rates are so reasonable and they have a reputation for serving huge portions of delicious food?

14) Koloa Fish Market

Even food snobs give this modest eatery near the Koloa Post Office excellent praise despite its complete lack of atmosphere (meal is served in plastic containers). Due to the fact that it is also a store, there is no seating and there are lengthy queues. Many vouch for their homemade wasabi cream sauce, which they genuinely prepare.

15) Gino's Brick Oven Pizza

This Italian restaurant, another institution, has been recognized for the quality of its salads and pizzas. On the island, they have three locations: Kalaheo, Kapaa, and Kapolei. Each one has a bar in addition to serving the typical Italian dishes.

Chapter 7:
Accommodation In Kauai

The lovely Hawaiian island of Kauai, commonly called the "Garden Isle," is well-known for its breathtaking natural scenery and outdoor pursuits. In terms of lodging selections, Kauai has a variety to accommodate various spending limits and tastes. Here are some popular lodging options you may want to think about in Kauai:

1. Hotels and Resorts: The eastern and southern shores of the island of Kauai are home to a number of opulent hotels and resorts. These lodgings include a variety of facilities like proximity to lovely beaches, restaurants, and spas.

2. Vacation rentals: Renting a villa, condo, or vacation house is a common decision in Kauai. Through vacation rental websites or neighborhood property management firms, you can find a variety of possibilities. Vacation rentals are perfect for families and bigger groups since they frequently offer extra room, privacy, and amenities like kitchens and laundry rooms.

3. Bed and Breakfasts: The towns of Hanalei, Poipu, and Kapaa are home to several delightful bed and breakfast establishments on Kauai. These more intimate lodgings frequently provide individualized service, a hearty breakfast, and a welcoming atmosphere.

4. Hostels & Low-Cost Accommodations: Kauai also boasts a few hostels and low-cost lodging options if your vacation budget is limited. These alternatives often include individual rooms or dormitory-style rooms at reasonable prices.

5. Camping: Kauai offers options for camping in specified campgrounds for intrepid tourists. Camping gives you the chance to fully appreciate the island's natural splendor, albeit permits are needed and amenities can vary.

Think about things like location, amenities, closeness to activities, and your budget when selecting your lodging. To guarantee your favorite choice, it's also a good idea to make reservations in advance, especially during the busiest travel season.

Hotels and Resorts

These top 10 Kauai hotels and resorts are renowned for their opulent lodgings, breathtaking settings, and first-rate services:

1. The St. Regis Princeville Resort: This opulent resort, which is located on the North Shore, features a world-class golf course, a spa, and spectacular ocean views. It creates a lavish and peaceful environment.
2. Grand Hyatt Kauai Resort and Spa: This luxurious resort is situated in Poipu and offers a large tropical garden, a saltwater lagoon, various pools, and a full-service spa. It provides a variety of eating options and opulent lodging.
3. Koa Kea Hotel & Resort: This boutique hotel, which is tucked away on Poipu Beach, offers a cozy and peaceful environment. It provides a magnificent and individualized experience with well-appointed suites, dining options on the oceanfront, and an outstanding spa.
4. Princeville Resort Kauai: This hotel underwent renovations and now offers breathtaking views of Hanalei Bay and the surrounding mountains. It was formerly known as the renowned St. Regis Princeville. It has upmarket lodging, a golf course, and a selection of restaurants.
5. The Lodge at Kukui'ula: This opulent resort, which is located in the posh Kukui'ula neighborhood, provides individual cottages and plantation-style residences with

access to priceless extras like a private golf course, spa, and farm-to-table dining options.

6. Ko'a Kea Hotel & Resort: This boutique hotel on Poipu Beach offers stylish accommodations, a tranquil pool area, and easy access to the beach. It offers a luxurious and serene retreat.

7. Kauai Beach Resort: This oceanfront resort on Kauai's eastern shore features large accommodations, numerous pools, waterslides, and a full-service spa. It offers a welcoming environment for families and easy access to the airport.

8. Sheraton Kauai Resort: This Poipu Beach resort offers lovely seaside views, cozy accommodations, and a variety of eating options. It provides a tranquil, welcoming atmosphere for families.

9. Hanalei Bay Resort: This resort, which overlooks the well-known Hanalei Bay, has breathtaking views, roomy accommodations, and a peaceful environment. It offers tennis courts, a sizable pool, and access to a private beach.

10. Timbers Kauai - Hokuala: This opulent resort, which sits on Kauai's southeast coast, features oceanfront homes, a Jack Nicklaus golf course, and a range of leisure pursuits. It offers a luxurious, exclusive experience.

These Kauai hotels and resorts are renowned for their first-rate service, picturesque settings, and opulent amenities, guaranteeing a delightful stay on the Garden Island.

Vacation Rentals

The island offers a variety of vacation rental styles to accommodate various tastes and price ranges. Here are a few typical choices:

1. Vacation Homes: Cozy cottages and opulent beachfront houses are also available on Kauai's rental market. These houses are fully furnished and with features like private pools, gardens, BBQ pits, and breathtaking views of the beach or mountains. Vacation houses are perfect for families or bigger groups since they offer privacy and space.

2. Condos and Apartments: Apartments and condos are popular options for vacation rentals in Kauai. These accommodations, which often include swimming pools, exercise centers, and on-site eateries, are found in resorts or housing developments. Condos and apartments are available in a range of sizes, from studios to multi-bedroom homes, and frequently have balconies or lanais to take in the spectacular views of the island.

3. Cottages and Bungalows: When visiting Kauai, think about staying in a cottage or bungalow for a warm and private

experience. These more compact lodgings provide a tranquil getaway and are frequently tucked away in beautiful tropical environments. They are ideal for couples or lone tourists seeking a peaceful retreat amidst nature or a romantic getaway.

4. Villas: Numerous opulent villas on Kauai offer a high-end holiday experience. These homes are frequently large and equipped with expensive features including gourmet kitchens, private pools, and many bedrooms. For a truly luxurious stay, villas frequently include extra amenities like private chefs, housekeeping, and concierge help.

5. Eco-Lodges: The eco-lodges on Kauai show the island's dedication to environmental preservation and ecotourism. For tourists who are concerned about the environment, these lodgings offer a distinctive experience that blends in seamlessly with the island's natural surroundings. Eco-lodges frequently place a high priority on environmentally friendly procedures and give visitors access to outdoor activities.

Think about things like location, amenities, price range, and the size of your group when selecting a vacation rental in Kauai. To reserve your favorite rental and make the most of your trip to this lovely Hawaiian island, make your reservations well in advance, especially during the busiest traffic times.

Camping options Here are some of the best camping options in Kauai:

1. Koke'e State Park: This park, which is found on the western side of the island, provides a variety of camping options surrounded by lush vegetation and spectacular views of Waimea Canyon.
2. Hanakapiai Beach: This quiet beach offers camping chances for hikers and backpackers looking for an adventure along the illustrious Kalalau Trail on the Na Pali Coast.
3. Polihale State Park: A lengthy stretch of immaculate beach and camping areas with expansive views of the ocean and the Na Pali Coast are available at Polihale, which is located on the western shore of the island.
4. Anini Beach Park: This beach area, which located on the north shore, offers a relaxing camping experience with calm waves, a stunning reef, and lots of shelter from ironwood trees.
5. Salt Pond Beach Park: This beach park is situated near Hanapepe and offers a campground with ocean views, amenities, and a swimming pond with natural seawater.
6. Camp Sloggett: This campground, which is tucked away in the Koke'e Mountains, provides a tranquil haven with access to hiking trails and breathtaking views of the interior of the island.

7. Nāmāhoana Campsite: This isolated campground in Koke'e State Park offers peace and quiet for campers while being close to the Waimea Canyon and hiking paths.
8. Haena Beach Park: This beach park is situated on the north shore close to the well-known Na Pali Coast and provides camping with stunning views, simple access to Tunnels Beach, and surrounding hiking opportunities.

Before organizing a camping trip in Kauai, don't forget to verify the availability, permits, and any restrictions.

Chapter 8:
Shopping and Souvenirs in Kauai

With a variety of things to consider, this can be a joyful experience. Whether you're looking for local crafts, unique souvenirs, or high-end boutiques, there are plenty of shopping opportunities on the island. Here are some of the well-liked stores on Kauai:

1. Poipu Shopping Village: This open-air shopping mall, which is situated in Poipu's resort district, features a number of shops, including apparel boutiques, art

galleries, jewelry stores, and gift shops. Additionally, there are live performances and dining alternatives nearby.

2. Kukui Grove Center: The biggest shopping center on the island, Kukui Grove Center, is located in Lihue. It has a mix of regional and national businesses, including clothes boutiques, spas, bookstores, and movie theaters. On specific days, you may also find local goods and fresh produce at the farmer's market.

3. Hanapepe Town: Hanapepe, also referred to as Kauai's "largest little town," is a quaint historic village with a number of art galleries, gift shops, and specialized businesses. It's a terrific location for discovering original artwork, regional crafts, and antiques. Don't miss Friday night's Hanapepe Art Night, where you can peruse galleries, take in live music, and savor gourmet vendors.

4. Kauai Products Fair: This market, which is in Lihue, features a selection of locally produced goods and artwork created by Kauai craftsmen. Along with other things, you can find handmade jewelry, clothes, artwork, and food items. It's a terrific spot to shop locally and find genuine Kauai trinkets.

5. Princeville Center: Visitors staying in the Princeville region frequently travel to the island's North Shore to shop at Princeville Center. It provides a range of specialty stores, eateries, and boutiques. Beachwear and outdoor gear are also available here.

6. Local Farmers' Markets: It is essential to attend the neighborhood farmers' markets because Kauai is renowned for its abundance of fresh vegetables. Particularly well-liked markets include the Hanalei Farmers Market and the Kauai Community Market in Lihue. A broad variety of fresh farm products are available, including fruits, vegetables, baked goods, local honey, and other foods.

Keep in mind to double-check each location's hours of operation because they could change. Additionally, buying genuine Kauai items is a great way to support regional companies and craftspeople.

Souvenirs to buy.

There are a number of mementos you might think about bringing home from Kauai to remember your stay. Here are a few well-liked choices:

1. Kukui Nut Jewelry: Native to Hawaii, kukui nuts are frequently used to create stunning necklaces, bracelets, and earrings. They are special and significant keepsakes.
2. Hawaiian Quilts: Hawaiian quilts are famous for being complex and vibrant in Kauai. These carefully hand-made quilts frequently have traditional Hawaiian designs. They might make lovely, useful souvenirs of your journey.

3. Macadamia NutsHawaii is well-known for its macadamia nuts, and Kauai is home to several of these farms. To take some wonderful souvenirs home, you can purchase bags of macadamia nuts that have been roasted, spiced, or wrapped in chocolate.

4. Kauai Coffee: There are some outstanding coffee estates on the island of Kauai, and their coffee is well-known. For a sense of the island long after your visit, buy locally grown and roasted Kauai coffee beans or ground coffee.

5. Tropical Fruit Products: The lush climate of Kauai produces mouthwatering tropical fruits. Look for items like passion fruit syrup, mango chutney, or pineapple jam. These products are wonderful gifts and capture the flavors of the island.

6. Hawaiian Shirts or Dresses: Hawaiian shirts (also known as "aloha shirts") or Hawaiian dresses are traditional keepsakes from any vacation to Hawaii (known as a muumuu). These colorfully printed clothes are excellent for bringing the island's carefree attitude home with you.

7. Island Artwork: There is a strong artistic culture on Kauai, and the island serves as inspiration for a wide range of works of art. Look for artwork that beautifully depicts the scenery, vegetation, and fauna of Kauai in paintings, prints, or sculptures.

8. Shell Jewelry: The beaches on Kauai are a seashell collector's paradise. You can purchase shell bracelets,

earrings, or necklaces that highlight the island's natural beauty.

9. Hawaiian Music: Purchase or download some Hawaiian music performed by regional musicians. Every time you listen to them, the calming melodies and rhythms will bring back memories of Kauai.

To make sure you adhere to the essential standards, remember to verify local laws and customs restrictions governing the shipping of specific items, notably food products or plant materials.

Conclusion

If you were considering visiting Kauai this year, which you really should, this thorough travel guide would provide you all the information you need.

If your trip is properly planned, you can unwind and avoid worry at the last minute.

In terms of weather, people, demand, and cost, keep in mind that April, May, August, September, October, and November are the ideal months to visit Kauai. Enjoy!

Snorkle Tour
kayak Tour

Made in United States
Troutdale, OR
06/11/2023

10565076R00066